Garden Toes

Written and Illustrated by Peggy Nolan
Collage Design by Terry Dostalik

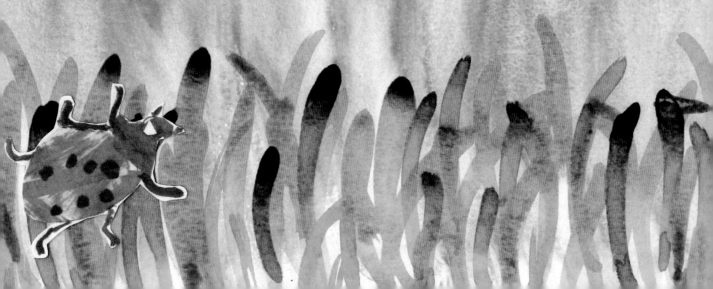

For audio go to Gardentoes.com

In Gratitude

To Brian and our Camping Trips

To the Neptune Beach Children's Garden
Community

And to Children in Gardens Everywhere

Peggy

Garden Toes

Garden Toes

Look at my Garden Toes

Brown from the soil

Green on its way

Sow some seeds

Sprouts any day!

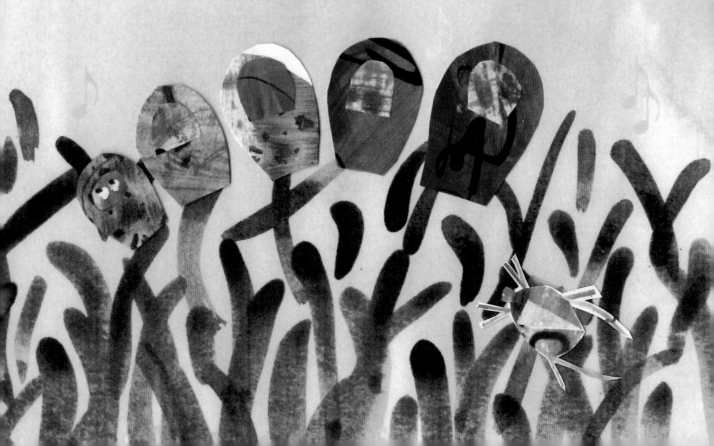

Soil is smiling
Garden says
Good Day!

Sun heats up
Rain is on its way.
I like my feet bare
I feel the Earth
She talks with me and
I'm part of her worth.

Oh, oh, Yeah...

Garden Toes

Garden Toes

Look at my Garden Toes

Brown from the Soil

Green on its way

Sow some seeds

Sprouts any day!

I plant and I water
and sometimes I weed

My Garden Toes show me
what the Garden needs.

I walk around
My Toes lead the way

The Garden invites
The Toes to play.

Oh, oh, Yeah...

Garden Toes

Garden Toes

Look at my Garden Toes

Brown from the Soil

Green on its way

Sow some seeds

Sprouts any day!

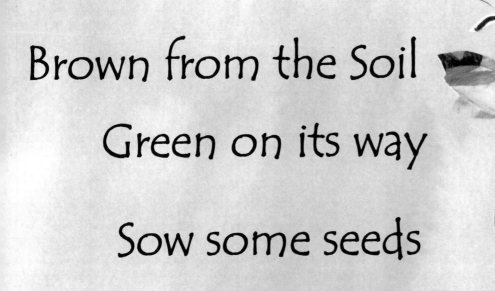

Living in the Garden
Insects abound
Helpers and Eaters
Enough to go around.

Oh, oh, Yeah...

Garden Toes
Garden Toes

Look at my Garden Toes

Brown from the Soil
Green on its way

Sow some seeds
Sprouts any day!

Toes wake up!
The Garden's green

Trot to the backyard
to find a bean.

Squash is coming

So is corn

Toes are sprouting

This early morn.

Oh, oh, Yeah...

Garden Toes, Garden Toes
Look at my Garden Toes

Brown from the Soil
Green on its way

Sow some seeds
Sprouts any day!

Good night,
Garden Toes!

The End

Foot Facts

The human foot has 26 bones, 33 joints, 107 ligaments and 19 muscles and tendons.

Your footprint is unique to you, just like your handprint.

There are thousands of exteroceptors (sensory receptors that gather information from outside the body) in the sole of each foot.

Going barefoot is healthy for your skin, providing ventilation. The increased sensory information protects the foot as well as the bones and joints.

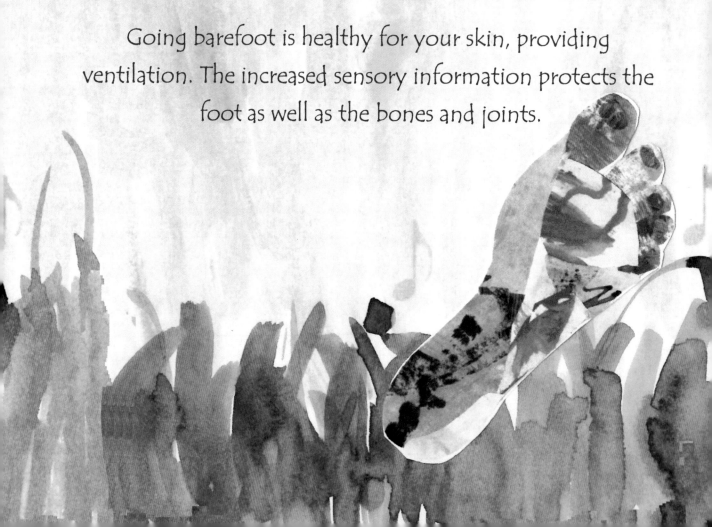

Trace your Garden Toes (and Foot) here!
Who else lives in the Garden with you?

Are your Garden Toes sprouting yet?

Peggy Nolan, after spending decades as a teacher in

Montessori and Waldorf classrooms, has found her happiest

place singing in the garden while growing fruits, vegetables

and herbs and eating wonderful healthy harvests. This

includes, of course, sharing the bounty with children and

families in the local community. She and her sister Terry

Dostalik, gardener and artist, both live in Atlantic Beach,

Florida and consider the beaches an amazing place to work

and play.

Made in the USA
Columbia, SC
27 March 2018